To Steve, Zo, Lila and Dex.
– M.R.

Special thanks to Maria for being there for me,
to David for his unconditional support and to you, Gim.
– N.T.

SEASON
of the
WITCH

Written by Matt Ralphs   Illustrated by Núria Tamarit

FLYING EYE

LONDON | NEW YORK

CONTENTS

A MAGICAL GATHERING

Dusk falls like a soft blanket over the forest clearing.
The air is warm and filled with magic. A gathering of
people murmur secrets and swap spells. A woman
snaps her fingers, bringing a campfire to life. Birds and
animals fall silent and even the stars seem to listen. It is
time for the witches and sorcerers to tell their tales.

From ancient magic-users in Mesopotamia to modern-day Wiccans, people have believed in magic for thousands of years. Nearly every culture throughout history had their own special magical beliefs, traditions and practices. But what exactly *is* magic?

Magic was a powerful force to be feared and respected—invisible but ever-present. Some ancient cultures thought that if they left gifts at temples, their gods and goddesses would share their magic in the form of blessings. Others believed magic was a force that could be harnessed by magic-users themselves.

Magic-users have gone by many names throughout the centuries: witches, warlocks, sorceresses, wizards and shamans to name only a few. They believed they could use spells, potions and magical ceremonies for good or bad purposes, such as telling the future or laying on curses.

We'll begin 5,000 years ago at the birth of human civilization in the Middle East, where magician-priests used their skills to heal the sick. Follow magic's silver thread through history to visit fierce Norse sorceresses, spell-muttering Medieval witches, Vodou charm-casters and many more. We'll also explore some of these cultures' magical myths and most famous magic-users.

So, get comfy, turn the page, and begin your journey into the magical world of witches!

ANCIENT MESOPOTAMIAN MAGIC

310–500 BCE

The sun is setting. A warm desert breeze hisses through the bulrushes on the banks of the Tigris River. Inside a hut filled with the scent of incense, a woman lies stricken by sickness. Beside her sits a man mixing a potion and whispering an incantation to the great god, Ea.

Welcome to Mesopotamia

From the Taurus Mountain in what is now southern Turkey, two mighty rivers flow: the Tigris and Euphrates. Between these rivers lies the fertile land of Mesopotamia, where the first human civilizations started 5,000 years ago. These cultures invented the first written languages, built huge cities, and traveled far and wide. They also held a strong belief in magic.

Learned magicians

The people who practised magic in Mesopotamia were called "ašipu," meaning "exorcist": someone who drives away evil spirits. In this culture, only men were allowed to practice magic. Ašipu were highly respected scholars and doctors, who tried to cure illnesses by fighting the evil magic they believed had caused them. They spent their lives studying their art and praying to Ea, the Mesopotamian god of magic and medicine (see page 12).

Medical magic

The ašipu used magic for many things: warding off evil spells created by other magic-users, repelling ghosts or soothing a vengeful god's anger. Once they diagnosed a sickness, the ašipu attempted to cure the sufferer using a mixture of medicine, magical spells and prayers to Ea. The aim was to cleanse the patient's soul of the evil sorcery that had caused the disease. Although far less effective than modern medicine, it's possible that the ašipu's work had a generally helpful effect on the patient's mental and physical wellbeing.

A taste of their own medicine

For the ašipu, life was a constant battle between light and dark magic. While the ašipu used magic to help people, there were other sorcerers working in the shadows who used it for evil purposes. The ancient Mesopotamians thought dark magic was used to cause calamities, bad luck and sickness.

When disaster struck, people employed ašipu to draw the curse out from a victim of dark magic and send it back to the evil sorcerer, so they suffered the consequences instead.

EA

Lord of the Abzu

The Mesopotamians worshipped many gods and goddesses, but Ea was one of the most important. They believed he was the source of all magical wisdom.

Ea was something of a trickster. Legend tells that he used his cunning to outwit Enlil, the supreme god of the Mesopotamians. The story goes that while sitting at home in the Abzu, Ea's underground ocean realm, he was struck with the idea of creating something truly special. Using figures molded from clay, Ea created the human race. From that moment on, humanity served the gods and spread across the Earth in their multitudes.

Enlil became enraged with humanity's constant clamor as the noise of their lives made it impossible for him to sleep. Unable to withhold his anger, Enlil created a flood to sweep the lands and rid himself of the maddening humans.

But the clever Ea foresaw Enlil's murderous plan. Desperate to save his people from a watery doom, Ea ordered a man called Atrahasis to build a ship and invite all of humanity on board. When Enlil's flood rose to cover the whole face of the Earth, the boat lifted with it and the people were saved, all thanks to Ea, Lord of the Abzu.

WHAT A WITCH LOOKS LIKE

The classic witch in countless stories is an old woman wearing robes and a pointed hat, flying on a broomstick with her black cat companion. But wheredo these ideas come from?

Broomsticks

Witches are often portrayed flying through the sky. There are drawings from as far back as the year 1400 that show witches darting through the sky on broomsticks (also called "besoms").

The broomstick myth may have come from witches creating potions from strong-smelling ingredients. The potions affected the witch's mind, creating sensations that made them feel as if they were flying through the air. They applied these potions to their bodies with... a broomstick!

Pointed hats

In fairy tales and films, witches are nearly always seen wearing a black pointed hat. You might even have worn a hat like that yourself for Halloween. But why, of all the hats that have ever existed, is this the one associated with witches?

One theory dates back to the Middle Ages, when it was fashionable for women to wear a type of headdress called a "hennin". These were conical hats that were sometimes as tall as 30 inches! Around this time, the Catholic Church believed witches were usually women and that they gained their magical powers from the Devil. Priests may have made a connection between women's pointy hennins and the Devil's horns, which turned into a link between witches and pointed hats.

Green skin

The idea of green-skinned witches was born in 1939 with the film *The Wizard of Oz*. This was one of the first films to be made in color, and the film studio wanted to make full use of this new technology to impress the audience. So they added lots of color to the film, including giving the main character Dorothy ruby-red shoes, and the Wicked Witch of the West bright green skin. The idea that witches have green skin has stuck with us for over 80 years.

ANCIENT EGYPTIAN MAGIC

300–30 BCE

The midday sun glares, but the air remains cool inside the high-ceilinged temple with brightly painted walls. Sick people wait to be treated, some lying on beds covered with reeds. Among them walk the Priests of Heka, dispensing advice and medicine, and whispering spells to expel disease.

Welcome to Ancient Egypt

Under the rule of the Pharaohs, the ancient Egyptian civilization flourished for 3,000 years on the fertile banks of the Nile River. They built incredible cities, temples and pyramids and invented systems of writing, maths and medicine. Ancient Egyptians called magic "Heka". It was as much a part of everyday life as sleeping and eating, and was found in everything: air, water, rocks, plants, animals and trees.

The god of magic

The Ancient Egyptians believed that the god of magic, also named Heka (see page 18), used magic to create the entire universe. Heka was widely worshipped and is often mentioned in ancient Egyptian spells and medical texts. He is shown in art as a bearded man wearing royal garments and holding a staff entwined with two serpents, a symbol still associated with medicine today. Magic-users in ancient Egypt were called Priests of Heka. Their job was to cure the sick by using a combination of spells, prayers and medicine.

Practical priests

Priests of Heka had many practical skills, such as being able to fix broken bones and bind wounds. Like in ancient Mesopotamia, Priests of Heka were usually only men. They worked in magnificent temples that had dedicated areas for healing. Rolls made of papyrus (an early form of paper) were used to record information about illnesses and treatments, so the Priests had to be able to read and write, which was not common then.

Ancient advice

The Ebers Papyrus is one of the oldest medical texts in the world. It is over 65 feet long and contains treatments for bone fractures, burns and heart disease, as well as dentistry tips.

Priests of Heka used advice from the Ebers Papyrus that we still agree with now, for example, that people should eat healthy food. It also contained knowledge about the human body that remains remarkably accurate, such as the heart being the center of the body's blood supply. However, the scroll also says that the heart produces tears and urine, which is not true. Other advice is best avoided entirely, such as rubbing crocodile dung on your body to ward off evil spirits.

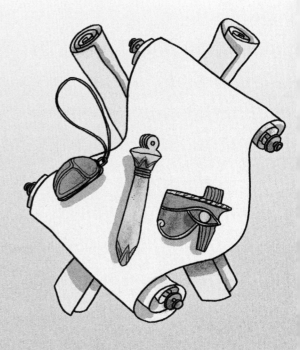

HEKA

God of magic

It is said that Heka, ancient god of magic, was present before the birth of all things. When the heavens, Earth, seas, people and animals were brought into existence from the swirling waters of chaos, it was Heka's magic that made it possible. The other gods feared and respected him, because they knew his strength and wisdom.

"To me belonged the universe before you came into being," he would say to the younger gods. "You have come afterwards, because I am Heka." Other gods and goddesses came and went, but Heka remained the one people turned to when they needed the power of magic to heal them. He brought their souls into existence, and after death, he made sure they traveled unharmed through the Underworld and into the Field of Reeds.

Heka traveled with the falcon-headed sun god Ra in his sacred boat. Every day they forged a fiery path across the heavens, and every night they plunged into the Underworld to do battle with demons. In the depths of that dreadful place, they faced the mighty snake demon Apep, Lord of Chaos and enemy of light. Apep tried to defeat them with his magical gaze and earthquake-causing roars. However, Heka and Ra were more powerful and defeated him every night, rising victorious at dawn to bring light and life to the people of Egypt.

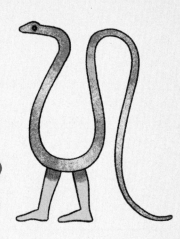

THE BOOKS OF THE DEAD

Journey to the afterlife

The ancient Egyptians believed in an afterlife called the Field of Reeds, a beautiful place where the souls of good people existed in blissful happiness forever. But getting there was not easy. After death, the soul had to find its way through a terrifying place under the earth called Duat, filled with demons, traps and fiery lakes. To help souls on this journey, the ancient Egyptians carved sections from the Books of the Dead onto tomb walls and inside coffins.

Bound by magic

The Books of the Dead were collections of papyrus leaves. On them were hieroglyphs, colourful drawings of gods, demon-warding spells and maps showing the safe routes through Duat. Many different versions were written over the centuries. Some Books of the Dead were simple, others beautiful and created by masterful artists, but all were meant to be used by the souls of the dead to navigate Duat and reach the Hall of Judgement.

Light as a feather

Osiris, god of the underworld, ruled over the Hall of Judgement. He took a person's heart and weighed it against a feather on the Scales of Justice. If the heart was pure and balanced the scales, the soul was allowed into the Field of Reeds. If the heart was evil and weighed more than the feather, it was eaten by Ammut, devourer of the dead. This condemned the soul to wander Duat for eternity. Below is a spell of protection taken from the Book of the Dead, to be spoken by souls on their journey through Duat:

Make way for me, that I may see **Amun.**
For I am that **Akh** who passes by the guards.
I am equipped and effective in opening his **portal.**
As for any person who knows this spell, he will be like **Ra**
in the eastern sky, like Osiris in the underworld.
He will go down to the Circle of Fire,
without the flame touching him ever.

Amun — king of the gods
Akh — soul
Portal — door
Ra — god of the sun

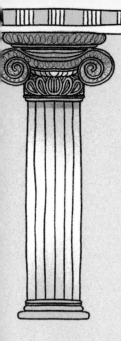

ANCIENT GREEK MAGIC

800–146 BCE

The sky is dark and studded with stars. The sounds of the Mediterranean Sea carry on the warm breeze. A woman kneels before a shrine to Hecate. She whispers a prayer of protection for her unborn child. Hecate's statue looks down on her, listening.

Welcome to Ancient Greece

The ancient Greeks achieved many amazing things: they built tremendous cities, temples and aqueducts and laid the foundations of Western democracy. Their time may have ended millennia ago, but their scientific, philosophical and artistic legacy is still with us today.

Alongside new ways of thinking, a belief in magic was still part of their daily lives. The Greeks used spells, amulets and potions, and visited fortune-tellers to learn of their future. Magical inscriptions were carved onto city walls to protect them from disaster. Ordinary people believed they could gain control of magic by bargaining directly with the gods.

Gods and goddesses

Magic and religion were closely tied together in ancient Greece. People worshipped many gods and goddesses, but the deities most associated with magic were wing-footed Hermes, Moon-goddess Hecate and Circe the sorceress.

The relationship between a person and a god was one of give-and-take: the deity provided luck, health and prosperity, but only after payment had been made. People prayed and gave ritual offerings of food and wine, either at a temple or in their homes, to be blessed with a deity's favour. In a world of danger and disease, talking to gods and goddesses using magic and prayer gave people a sense of control over their lives.

Magical jewelry

Magical amulets were a type of good luck charm often worn as necklaces or bracelets. They were made from wood, stone, animal bones and even semi-precious gemstones, for those who could afford it. Sometimes people wrote spells on papyrus and wore them in a pouch around their necks. They believed these amulets had magical properties bestowed on them by the gods and goddesses. It was thought that wearing one could cure illness, bring good luck, keep robbers at bay or give you strength if you were an athlete or soldier.

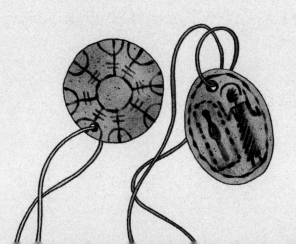

23

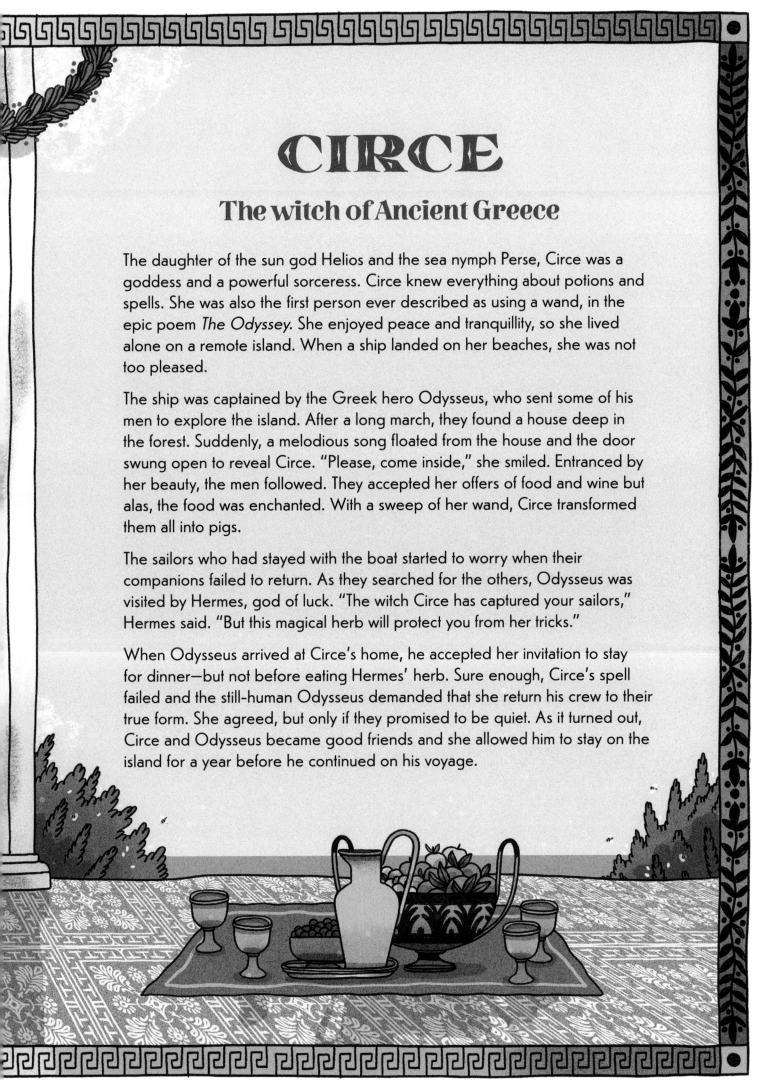

CIRCE

The witch of Ancient Greece

The daughter of the sun god Helios and the sea nymph Perse, Circe was a goddess and a powerful sorceress. Circe knew everything about potions and spells. She was also the first person ever described as using a wand, in the epic poem *The Odyssey*. She enjoyed peace and tranquillity, so she lived alone on a remote island. When a ship landed on her beaches, she was not too pleased.

The ship was captained by the Greek hero Odysseus, who sent some of his men to explore the island. After a long march, they found a house deep in the forest. Suddenly, a melodious song floated from the house and the door swung open to reveal Circe. "Please, come inside," she smiled. Entranced by her beauty, the men followed. They accepted her offers of food and wine but alas, the food was enchanted. With a sweep of her wand, Circe transformed them all into pigs.

The sailors who had stayed with the boat started to worry when their companions failed to return. As they searched for the others, Odysseus was visited by Hermes, god of luck. "The witch Circe has captured your sailors," Hermes said. "But this magical herb will protect you from her tricks."

When Odysseus arrived at Circe's home, he accepted her invitation to stay for dinner—but not before eating Hermes' herb. Sure enough, Circe's spell failed and the still-human Odysseus demanded that she return his crew to their true form. She agreed, but only if they promised to be quiet. As it turned out, Circe and Odysseus became good friends and she allowed him to stay on the island for a year before he continued on his voyage.

WANDS AND FAMILIARS

Wands

A medieval spell book called the *Key of Solomon* describes a wand as an important part of a witch's kit. Wands have been used through history by certain witches to channel and focus magic, but they weren't used as widely as you might think. Most witches created magic with only potions, rituals and spells. Wands are still used today by many witches including Wiccans, which we will learn more about later in the book.

The wand itself does not contain magic. Magic comes from the witch, and the wand is used to channel it in a specific direction. Wands can also be used to gain power over spirits. They come in all shapes and sizes—some are simple wooden sticks with leather-bound handles, others are more decorative, with glass or metal ends. As well as being used to weave magic, the wand is a visible symbol of the witch's power.

Familiars

Being a witch could be lonely. Although they were respected for their magical services, many witches were considered outsiders in their community. Familiars are magical spirits who take on animal form: cats, dogs, goats, toads, ferrets, hares, rabbits, and even flies. Witches with familiars gained an important friend and companion as well as the familiar's magical knowledge. According to some magical traditions, familiars choose the witch they want as their companion. If the witch agrees, they spend the rest of their lives together.

SLAVIC MAGIC
50–1000 CE

A woman walks through the Belorussian forest while reading from a book. She enters a flower-filled clearing drenched in sunlight. Butterflies fill the air. She finds the mushrooms she needs and waits. Only when the sun has reached its peak does she harvest them.

Welcome to Eastern Europe

The Slavic people of the early Middle Ages lived in the vast plains and forests of Eastern Europe. Their magical beliefs came out of their storytelling and fairy tales, which often involved witches, magical creatures and demons. They believed magic-wielding was a skill that, with enough practice and study, everyone could learn and master. Casting spells, mixing potions and reading the future—sometimes by studying the shape of clouds or the flight patterns of birds— were open for all to try. Anyone with the desire and willingness to learn could become a witch.

Creature comforts

Magical creatures were also a part of everyday life and often came to live in peoples' homes. Long-nosed Kikimoras were thought to live behind stoves or in cellars. If the family who lived there fed the Kikimora, the creature would help around the house. But if it went hungry, it would smash plates and make a terrible racket at night, waking up everyone in the house.

Gathering herbs

Spells and potions were used by Slavic witches to cure disease, ease childbirth, summon spirits and even shapeshift. A potion's ingredients were of the utmost importance, but so was the way they were harvested. Timing was crucial. The sun's position in the sky at the moment of harvest affected how well the ingredients worked, as did the tool used to cut them. For example, herbs picked on Midsummer's Eve were especially powerful, so witches reserved that day to gather ingredients for the coming months.

Looks that could kill

Some people were believed to be born with an extraordinary magical ability—the Evil Eye. With this power, a person could supposedly cause injury or even death with just a glance. People were terrified of falling victim to the Evil Eye, and often accused defenseless people of using it, such as the disabled, people with physical deformities, and unmarried or widowed women. One Slavic folktale tells of a man who was so afraid he had the "gift" of the Evil Eye, he blinded himself to protect his children from harm.

BABA YAGA

The Iron-toothed Witch

A young girl called Natasha lived with her father, who loved her, and her stepmother, who hated her. One day the stepmother told Natasha to visit her sister, who lived deep in the forest. When Natasha found her aunt's house, she was amazed to discover that it stood on giant chicken legs.

The strange house's door was thrown open by a fearsome old woman with a mouth full of iron teeth. Natasha knew at once that this was Baba Yaga, a legendary witch who roasted and ate children. Her stepmother had sent her into a trap! Screeching with laughter, Baba Yaga locked Natasha in a room and went to stoke the oven. In the room was a skinny cat. Being a caring girl, Natasha gave it some cheese.

Grateful for the food, the cat said, "My mistress will chase you if you run away, but throw this magic comb in her path and you might escape." Natasha took the comb, thanked the cat, and climbed out through the window. When Baba Yaga realised her dinner was escaping, she clambered inside a giant mortar from her kitchen and flew off in pursuit.

As the cackling witch got closer, Natasha threw the comb behind her and it instantly grew into a thicket of trees so dense that even Baba Yaga couldn't force her way through. Screaming with rage, the witch returned home hungry and disappointed. When Natasha told her father what had happened, he threw the stepmother out and they lived happily ever after.

CAULDRONS AND POTIONS

Cauldrons

Most witches had big pots called cauldrons to brew potions in. Some cauldrons are set on three feet, some are placed over the fire on stands and some hang from chains. Light a blaze beneath and the flames lick the cauldron's sides to heat the contents. A witch can then add ingredients, stir the mixture, mutter a spell and then finally decant the finished potion into bottles.

The Battersea Cauldron

This cauldron was discovered in London's River Thames in 1861 and is now kept in the British Museum. It was forged 3,000 years ago during the Iron Age, from seven sheets of bronze. It has two handles and a rim with many ridges to make it strong. Witches used bubbling cauldrons just like this one to mix potions and healing medicines, but they were also used for everyday cooking. Patches and repairs on the Battersea Cauldron show it was used for generations, passed down from one owner to the next.

Potions

Potions had many uses, like making someone fall in love or putting a curse on them. Most potions were made using plants and roots. Witches harvested their ingredients from forests and fields or bought them from an apothecary (similar to a pharmacy).

Nettles
for joint and muscle pain.

Mugwort
for pain relief and digestive problems.

Fennel
for backache, coughs and bronchitis.

Crab-apples
for diarrhea.

Some ancient medicinal potions have been proven by modern scientists to actually work, but others would have had no effect. Here are some of the stranger ingredients used:

Animals
Animals parts used in potions include bat and pigeon blood, sparrow brains and the bones of toads that have been eaten by rats.

Mandrake root
Used for many potions including poisons and love tonics. Mandrake roots look strangely like a human figure, and were even said to scream when dug up.

Dung
Animal poop was used as well as body parts: dog dung for sore throats, ox dung for fevers and sheep dung for jaundice. While odd, some droppings do actually contain antibiotic properties, so there is method in the madness.

Human remains
Most gruesome of all was the use of human ingredients. Headaches were treated with powdered skull, human hair was used for curses and love potions, and human fat was rubbed onto sore joints.

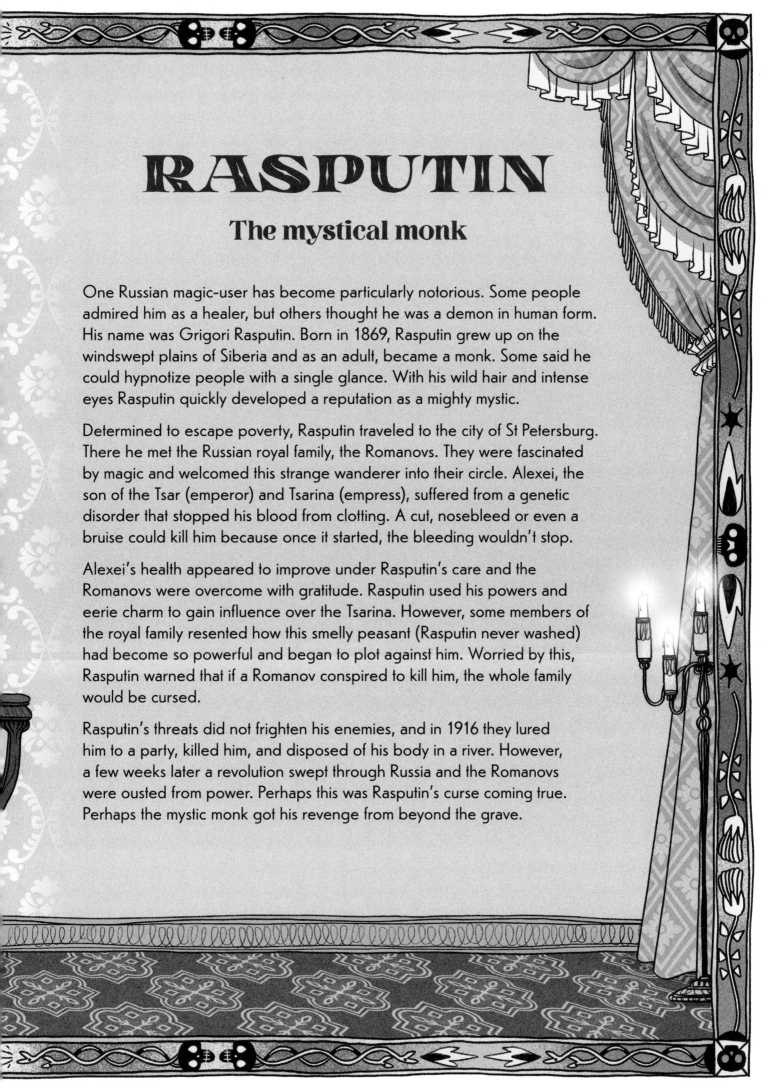

RASPUTIN

The mystical monk

One Russian magic-user has become particularly notorious. Some people admired him as a healer, but others thought he was a demon in human form. His name was Grigori Rasputin. Born in 1869, Rasputin grew up on the windswept plains of Siberia and as an adult, became a monk. Some said he could hypnotize people with a single glance. With his wild hair and intense eyes Rasputin quickly developed a reputation as a mighty mystic.

Determined to escape poverty, Rasputin traveled to the city of St Petersburg. There he met the Russian royal family, the Romanovs. They were fascinated by magic and welcomed this strange wanderer into their circle. Alexei, the son of the Tsar (emperor) and Tsarina (empress), suffered from a genetic disorder that stopped his blood from clotting. A cut, nosebleed or even a bruise could kill him because once it started, the bleeding wouldn't stop.

Alexei's health appeared to improve under Rasputin's care and the Romanovs were overcome with gratitude. Rasputin used his powers and eerie charm to gain influence over the Tsarina. However, some members of the royal family resented how this smelly peasant (Rasputin never washed) had become so powerful and began to plot against him. Worried by this, Rasputin warned that if a Romanov conspired to kill him, the whole family would be cursed.

Rasputin's threats did not frighten his enemies, and in 1916 they lured him to a party, killed him, and disposed of his body in a river. However, a few weeks later a revolution swept through Russia and the Romanovs were ousted from power. Perhaps this was Rasputin's curse coming true. Perhaps the mystic monk got his revenge from beyond the grave.

NORSE MAGIC
500–900 CE

A Norse village nestles at the top of a fjord. A crisp wind blows from the sea, ruffling the sails of the dragon-prowed ships. People stare as a young woman carrying a bronze-tipped staff strides through the village. She is a wandering sorceress, come to wield magic and foretell their future.

Welcome to Scandinavia

The Norse people of the Scandinavian Iron Age called magic "seidr" (pronounced SAY-der). Like many ancient societies, magic was closely related to religion. Gods and goddesses such as Thor, god of thunder, and Frigg, goddess of the sky, all practiced magic. Unlike the ancient cultures of Mesopotamia and Egypt, most magic-users in Scandinavia were women, perhaps because the deity most closely associated with magic was a goddess—Freya.

Norse witches

A Norse witch was called a völva, meaning "wand-carrier". They were highly respected in Norse society, specializing in sorcery and prophecy (fortune-telling). All völvur carried wands: long wooden staffs decorated with bronze and semi-precious stones. Völvur modelled themselves on the magical goddess Freya, and people went to them for their mysterious powers. The witches used potions and rituals to cure illness, bring good luck and find stolen items. Norse leaders employed völvur to bring good winds to sailors and give warriors courage before battle.

A völva's tools

Long blue cloaks
and dresses,
decorated with
gold thread

Fine jewelry

The wand was a völva's
most precious possession,
used to channel magic and
mark her out as a person
of high social class.

Leather waist bags
containing spell
ingredients such as
owl pellets, herbs
and animal bones

The power of foresight

The task of foretelling the future was done during
dramatic nighttime rituals. A völva could look
into the spirit realm by sitting on a high chair and
entering a trance. Women danced around her,
singing and banging drums. If their performance
pleased the spirits, they came forth and spoke to
the völva, helping her predict the future.

A völva could use her magic for good but also
for evil. She could cure illness but also cause it.
She could give a warrior strength, but also curse
him with weakness. This is why völvur were greatly
respected but also terribly feared.

SEA WITCHES

Magic-weaving water witches

During the worst sea storms, when dark waves crash onto Scandinavian shores, beware of eerie voices on the wind and pale faces beneath the water. For these are sea witches, powerful supernatural sorceresses as mysterious and unpredictable as the weather.

Sea witches share a sacred bond with the Moon and use their nimble fingers to turn lunar power into magic. Sailors treat sea witches with respect, knowing that at a moment's notice, a storm could rise up and sink their ship, controlled by the hand of a sea witch.

It is said that this happened in 1617, when a terrible hurricane struck the coast of Norway. So strong was the rain, that it seemed like the sea and sky had become one. So swift were the winds to rise, it was as if they'd been poured out from a huge bag. Fishing boats smashed on rocks or overturned, leaving the hulls belly-up under the thundery sky. Many sailors drowned in the North Sea that dark night.

The wives of the sailors managed to catch the sea witches in fishing nets and they confessed to causing the storm. However, before they could be executed, the witches slipped through their bonds and slid smoothly as eels back into the sea, cackling as they swam away.

SPELLS AND INCANTATIONS

The power of words

There are as many types of magic spell as there are fish in the sea. Spells can be whispered over a special object called a talisman to make it bring luck, or on a straw doll to lay on a curse. Spells can be shouted at the heavens to call down rain, or chanted in a magic circle to summon a demon.

Many witches use spells and incantations to wield magic. It is important to know that it's not only the words themselves that make the magic work, but how they are spoken. Pronunciation must be perfect, certain words may need to be emphasised and each spell requires a particular speed and rhythm. If you recite the spell incorrectly, it will fail.

The Key of Solomon

The *Key* was a spell book supposedly written by King Solomon, who ruled Israel sometime in the 10th century BCE. The earliest copies date from medieval times, centuries after King Solomon died. The book contains magical rituals, curses and ways to conjure spirits and demons. Shown below is part of an invisibility spell.

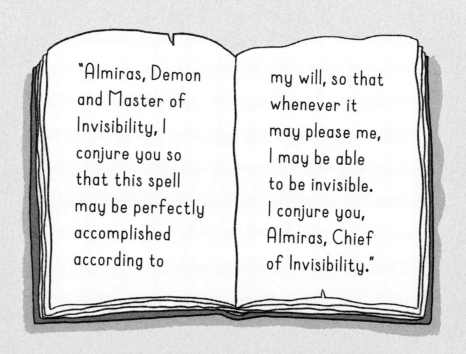

"Almiras, Demon and Master of Invisibility, I conjure you so that this spell may be perfectly accomplished according to my will, so that whenever it may please me, I may be able to be invisible. I conjure you, Almiras, Chief of Invisibility."

Abracadabra

Even if you are not a witch, most people's first thought when they think of a magic word is "Abracadabra". Abracadabra is a healing word that has been used for over 2,000 years. One urban legend says that during the Great Plague of London in 1665, people painted it on their doors in the hope that it would keep death away. To ward off sickness, an ancient Roman emperor called Caracalla wore an amulet around his neck with the word written in triangle form, as on the right.

It is unclear where the word comes from. It may be from the Aramaic (an ancient Middle Eastern language) words "Avrah KeDabra," which means "The magician's word will become reality." Or possibly from the Arabic words "Abra Kadabra," which mean "Let the things be destroyed"—the "things" in this case being sickness and disease.

```
A B R A C A D A B R A
A B R A C A D A B R
A B R A C A D A B
A B R A C A D A
A B R A C A D
A B R A C A
A B R A C
A B R A
A B R
A B
A
```

MEDIEVAL MAGIC
500-1500 CE

A simply furnished room is bathed in low evening light. Steam drifts from a cauldron, filling the air with the scent of nettles and thyme. Jars and pots line the shelves, and bundles of herbs hang from roof beams. A wise woman sits at a table, muttering spells as she mixes a potion in a bowl.

Welcome to Medieval Europe

The European Medieval period, also called the Middle Ages, was a time of progress and calamity, war and famine. In the mid-1300s the Black Death wiped out fifty percent of Europe's population, so it is unsurprising that Medieval people tried to use magic as a weapon against disease and death.

Although magic was carried out in a similar way to earlier periods, there was less emphasis on religion. Medieval Europe followed Catholicism, and the Catholic God was not associated with magic. However, witches sometimes mixed religious words in with their spells, even though the Catholic church called this heresy. Heresy was a disagreement with the church, a serious crime.

Cunning folk

Medieval society mostly valued magic-users and their services were widely used. Witches were called "cunning folk" in the Middle Ages. At that time "cunning" meant "knowledgeable," not "deceitful" or "crafty" as it does now. Every village and town had a cunning person, often an older woman with knowledge of herbs and simple magic spells. She treated the villagers' aches and pains, and sold good luck charms, health tonics and love potions.

On the outskirts

A witch's position in her community was complicated. They often provided the only medical treatment the average villager could afford, and their herb remedies could be effective. This made a witch valuable. However, some people feared their mysterious magical powers, so witches often lived alone. They were isolated from their community, and this made them vulnerable to accusations of using their magic for evil purposes.

Witch bottles

Some magic-users were accused of using dark magic to make people sick, turn milk sour (a big problem before fridges were invented) or ruining crops. Dark magic could be reversed with "witch bottles." To make a witch bottle, the cunning folk filled a bottle with bits of the victim's hair, fingernails and even urine, then held it over a fire. This supposedly destroyed the dark magic and caused terrible pain to the evil witch who had cast it.

MOTHER SHIPTON

The Yorkshire Seer

One night in 1488, a girl destined to become one of the most famous witches in England was born in a cave near the Yorkshire town of Knaresborough. Legend has it that her birth was greeted by a violent thunderstorm and the rotten egg smell of sulphur throughout the area. Her name was Ursula Shipton.

Ursula was not formed like most people. She had a large crooked nose, twisted legs and a bent back. The locals bullied her about her appearance, so she returned to the cave where she was born to escape their cruelty. There she learned the secrets of magic and how to use herbs to make medicines. Soon those same locals began to seek her out to cure their aches and pains.

Ursula became most famous for her ability to foresee the future. It is said that she predicted the Great Fire of London (1666) and the invention of iron ships (1830s). People visited her from miles around to ask about their fate, and she was given the name "Mother" because of the help and advice she gave. Taverns were named after her and two still exist—one in her hometown of Knaresborough. Her cave is still open to visitors, and a statue of her sits on a bench in Knaresborough's market place. There is even a species of moth native to Yorkshire called Mother Shipton, which has markings that look like a face.

GRIMOIRES

Word of mouth

A grimoire is a spell book filled with magical instructions. As Medieval witches were usually poor women living in the countryside with no formal education, most of them did not own any books. Instead they used word of mouth to share potion recipes, spells and magical knowledge with other witches, their families, and any apprentices or students they had.

Wealthy warlocks

Some Medieval magic-users did use spell books. They were usually wealthy male witches (called warlocks, sorcerers or wizards). Unlike most women at that time, men were allowed an education and could read the spells and potions contained in grimoires. They often displayed these precious books to impress their customers, although they had to be careful because grimoires were banned by the Catholic Church. Eventually, many years after the invention of the printing press in the 1450s, the Church allowed books on magic to be mass-produced. This gave many more people access to magical knowledge.

The Picatrix

Imagine being able to draw power from the Moon and using it to control nature. Or storing magic from a planet in a talisman to be used later, like money in the bank. Now, imagine calling forth supernatural spirits to do your bidding, or turning worthless substances into gold. Instructions to do all these things and more are found in a strange and wonderful grimoire called the *Picatrix*.

Written in Arabic in the 11th century, the *Picatrix* is a manual for witches and wizards that brings together magical knowledge from Egypt, Persia, India and the Middle East. Here is a magical ritual from the *Picatrix*, using magic from the Moon to make a field more fertile:

In a plate of silver create an image of a seated man surrounded by crops, trees and plants. This should be made beneath an Ascendant of Taurus, and the Moon passing from the Sun against Saturn. Bury this image, and all the plants and crops nearby will greatly increase and be preserved from the destruction of animals and tempests.

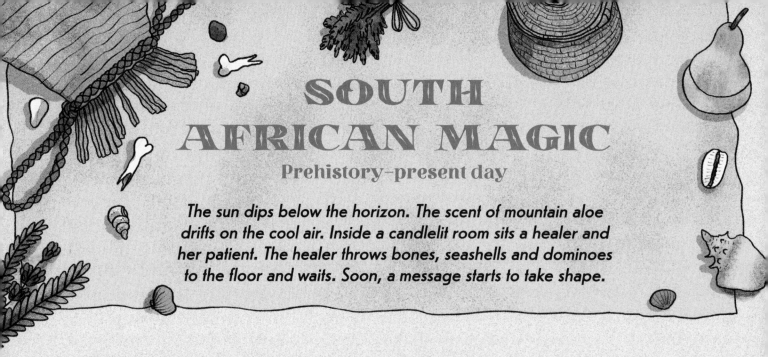

SOUTH AFRICAN MAGIC
Prehistory–present day

The sun dips below the horizon. The scent of mountain aloe drifts on the cool air. Inside a candlelit room sits a healer and her patient. The healer throws bones, seashells and dominoes to the floor and waits. Soon, a message starts to take shape.

Welcome to South Africa

Magic has been traditionally used for healing in South Africa for many hundreds of years, and still thrives to this day. South Africa is blessed with a huge diversity of plant life, which means that there is a particularly strong focus on herbs in the making of medicines and cures. Over 5,000 different species are used for healing purposes, and healers are experts in mixing the right ingredients. They can draw on centuries of knowledge and expertise to help their communities.

Keepers of knowledge

The practitioners of this ancient art are called sangomas. These highly respected men and women use herb medicine, rituals and spirit communication to treat their patients' illnesses, and share advice on life, health and love. Sangomas are not only skilled healers, but also councillors and keepers of sacred knowledge.

A call from the spirits

Not everyone can become a sangoma — the spirits must call a person to the role. The ancestral spirits communicate their wishes through strange dreams or visions. On accepting the call, the person first becomes a "twasa"—an apprentice. A long period of training begins, supervised by an experienced sangoma. The training includes:

- Learning how to foretell the future.
- Talking to spirits.
- Using herbs to create medicines.
- Local history and mythology.

A sangoma's toolkit

Every sangoma has a personal collection of objects, which often include animal bones, seashells, dominoes and dice. During a consultation, the sangoma throws these items on the floor, letting the spirits control where they land. The sangoma studies the way the items have fallen to interpret the spirit's message, and from this they work out how to treat the patient's ailment.

The arrangement of the fallen items (close together or far apart) and their individual positions (whether the domino is lying flat or on its edge) is very important. It can relate to the patient's health, happiness, mental state or future. Are they becoming ill? Are they depressed? What events are about to happen? Answers to these questions can be divined by the sangoma and told to their patient.

From Africa to the Americas
VODOU

Magic of many names

Vodou—also known as "voodoo" or "vodun"—is a religion and a way of seeing the world. Vodou means 'spirit' in the language of the ancient African kingdom of Dahomy (now called Benin). Practitioners of vodou believe in an invisible world populated by spirits, angels and the ghosts of their ancestors. These spirits are called "iwa" and have a strong influence over the lives of the living, so people offer them prayers in return for help.

The origins of vodou

Between 1500 and 1860, 12 million African men, women and children were stolen from their homes and sold into slavery to white Europeans and Americans. Thousands ended up working on the French colonial island of Haiti in the Caribbean.

As they worked to produce sugar, indigo dye and cotton, the enslaved people on Haiti took solace from their religions. Over time, these religions mixed with Catholic Christianity. This created vodou. After several slave revolts, the French were defeated and left the island. Many of the freed slaves went to America, taking vodou with them.

Letting the spirits in

To talk to the spirits and ask favours of them, vodou practitioners invite them to inhabit their own bodies. This is done at special ceremonies where the spirits are called forth using prayers, music and dance. The spirit speaks through the practitioner, giving advice, healing the sick and trying to fix any imbalances between the worlds of the living and the dead.

Brujeria

Similar beliefs to vodou are found in the Central American practice of brujeria. Like vodou, its roots originate in Africa and came over during the transatlantic slave trade. Brujeria is practiced by "brujo" (male practitioners) and "bruja" (female practitioners). They channel the spirits of the dead by entering the spirit world or inviting a spirit to possess them. Once this is done, the brujo or bruja can ask the spirit for advice or help in foretelling the future. They also make good luck charms, love spells and medicinal brews using herbs and magic spells.

MARIE LAVEAU

Vodou Queen of New Orleans

It's hard to distinguish where the legend ends and the facts begin when it comes to Marie Laveau. Born in 1801 in the vibrant American city of New Orleans, Marie was a free black woman who became a healer, fortune teller and the undisputed Vodou Queen of New Orleans.

A beautiful, statuesque woman with black hair and golden skin, she used her charisma to charm secrets and gossip from the highest levels of New Orleans society. The information Marie gathered and the powerful friends she made gave her a reputation as someone who knew everything about everyone and allowed her to earn a good living as a fortune-teller.

Inspired by her mother, Marie became a practitioner of Louisiana vodou, leading nighttime gatherings on Lake Pontchartrain and private seances in her house. Marie used her knowledge of magic to call forth spirits, often with her pet snake Zombi draped over her shoulders. These spirits whispered secrets to her and helped her foretell the future. Rich and poor alike visited Marie to buy lucky charms and potions, and to receive advice on love and life.

Marie's name is still heard in New Orleans today: gamblers call out her name for good luck when they throw the dice.

VODOU DOLLS
AND CHARMS

Vodou dolls

Enslaved West Africans in the Caribbean and the Americas brought their traditions with them. This included the use of vodou dolls. Similar magical dolls called "poppets" were used by Medieval European witches to curse people and cause them pain, but West Africans used vodou dolls for positive purposes. The dolls worked in a similar way to a talisman and could be used for healing. Vodou dolls could bounce back curses and were hung near cemeteries to help people talk with their dead loved ones.

Pwen

Vodouists (meaning "servants of the spirits") conjure spirits during their ceremonies to ask them about the future, or get advice on how to heal a sick patient. To draw the spirits out of their realm they use a pwen. These items hold a concentration of magical energy that the spirits are drawn to. Pwen come in many forms, but are often a human shaped doll. Some people think pwen are used for evil purposes such as laying on curses, but this is not true.

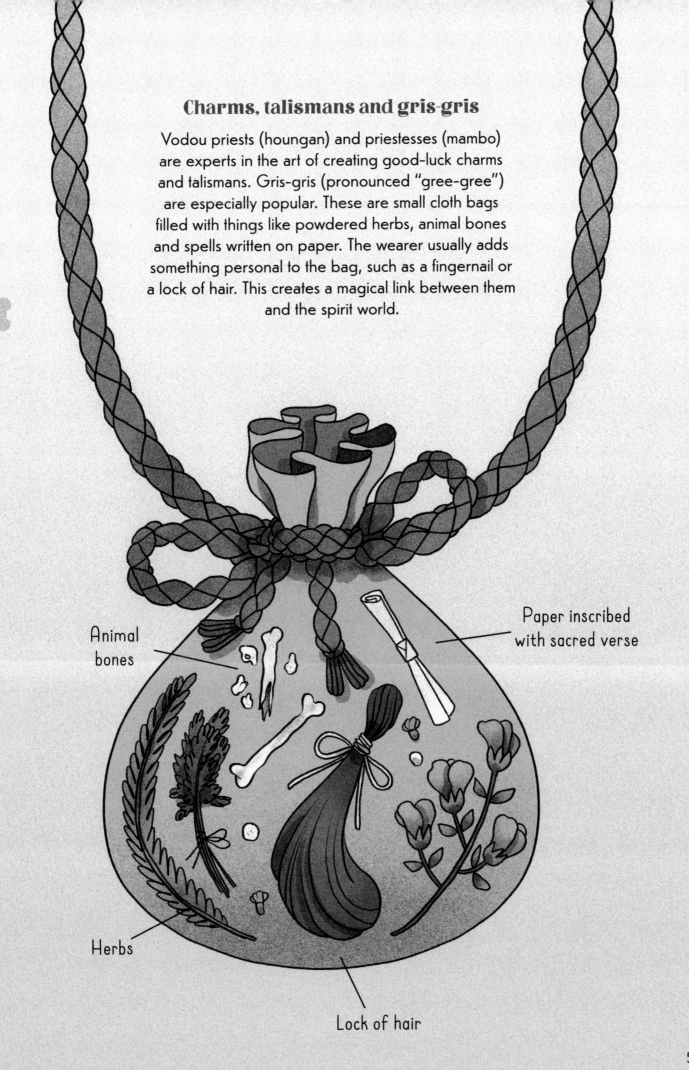

Charms, talismans and gris-gris

Vodou priests (houngan) and priestesses (mambo) are experts in the art of creating good-luck charms and talismans. Gris-gris (pronounced "gree-gree") are especially popular. These are small cloth bags filled with things like powdered herbs, animal bones and spells written on paper. The wearer usually adds something personal to the bag, such as a fingernail or a lock of hair. This creates a magical link between them and the spirit world.

Animal bones

Paper inscribed with sacred verse

Herbs

Lock of hair

JAPANESE MAGIC

600–present day

Pink blossom drifts through the trees, filling the air with perfume. A woman walks quietly. She has been searching for days and has grown weary... then she sees it. Resting on its side is a beautiful ocher-furred fox with— the woman quickly counts—nine tails. At last, her quest is over.

Welcome to Japan

Magic in Japan is closely connected to the world of spirits, the search for wisdom and yokai. Yokai are supernatural creatures that come in many forms: some are monstrous, some take the form of animals and others can almost pass for human. These creatures have magic that they wield for good or mischievous purposes, and Japanese witches befriend them to use it. They then use this magic for their benefit or for clients who pay for their services.

Witches and yokai

Many Japanese witches choose a fox-yokai to be their familiar. Fox-yokai, called kitsune, are wise creatures who live for a long time. You can tell how old and clever a kitsune is by counting its tails—the more it has, the better! A witch gains a kitsune familiar by befriending and feeding a pregnant vixen (a female kitsune). After giving birth, the vixen offers the witch one of her cubs by way of thanks. When the witch accepts the cub and names it, she takes the title kitsune-tsukai, which means "fox-user." The witch and kitsune can then travel together and use their combined magical skills.

A magical partnership

Once bound together, the witch uses the magical abilities of their kitsune to sell services to those in need. Kitsune can become invisible, allowing them to sneak about and discover secrets or recover stolen items. They can shape-shift into any human form they choose, fooling people into doing the witch's bidding.

A kitsune can also take possession of a person's mind and body. However, this is risky because the kitsune sometimes refuses to leave its host, resulting in permanent possession. With power such as this, it is no mystery why witches and their kitsune are treated with respect and caution.

Keeping it in the family

Sometimes entire witch families adopt a kitsune to take advantage of their invisibility, shape-shifting and spirit-possession magic. If the family treats their kitsune well (by feeding it lots of tofu, for example), they are repaid with wealth, good luck and prosperity. These fox-affiliated families, called kitsune-mochi, pass their familiar down from generation to generation, enjoying their abilities and blessings of luck.

YAMA-UBA
Crone of the mountains

When the sun dips low behind the jagged peaks of the Japanese mountains, lone travelers should beware. Stories tell of one such traveler who decided to explore the mountains many years ago. He walked for miles and miles until he was desperately tired and hungry. Just when he was about to turn home, a young woman stepped into his path. She smiled kindly and said, "I am Yama-uba. Would you like food and shelter for the night?"

The traveler eagerly agreed and followed Yama-uba into her hut. Yama-uba locked the door, turned around slowly and, before the traveler's horrified gaze, transformed into a terrifying witch with a sunken face and hair as wild and white as a blizzard. With a piercing shriek she leaped on him, her mouth wide and cavernous. By morning, there was nothing left of the traveler except gnawed bones...

Yama-uba had once been an ordinary young girl, but everything changed when famine struck her village. Rice paddy fields dried into dustbowls, food stocks dwindled to nothing and the people were left to eat grass and moss. In a desperate attempt to reduce the number of mouths to feed, Yama-uba's family abandoned her in the mountains.

Despite being lost and alone, Yama-uba survived and grew into a beautiful young woman. But her family's betrayal ate away at her mind, turning her monstrous. Legend has it that she still wanders the high mountains, waiting for unwary travelers who happen to pass by.

Magical Artifacts
HANNYA MASKS

Japanese folklore is full of stories of terrifying Hannya demons. These demons were once ordinary women who suffered such terrible heartbreak that the resulting jealousy and anger poisoned their minds and bodies, transforming them forever. There are three types of Hannya demon:

Namanari hannya
still retain their human form, except for two small horns sprouting from their heads.

Chūnari hannya
are more monstrous, with longer horns and tusks.

Honnari hannya
are the most dangerous and ferocious. They have serpent bodies and breathe fire.

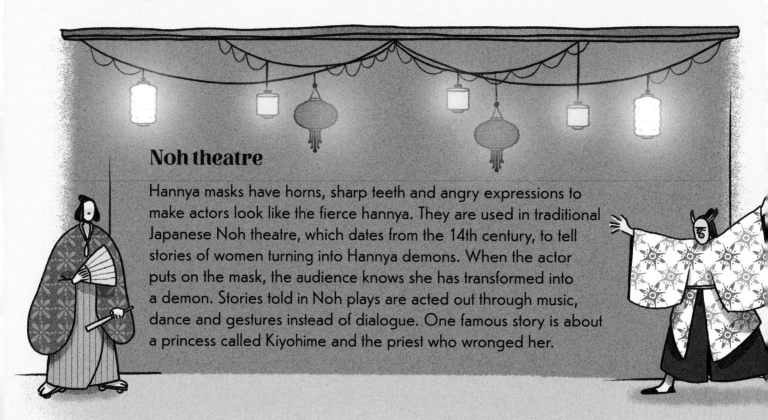

Noh theatre

Hannya masks have horns, sharp teeth and angry expressions to make actors look like the fierce hannya. They are used in traditional Japanese Noh theatre, which dates from the 14th century, to tell stories of women turning into Hannya demons. When the actor puts on the mask, the audience knows she has transformed into a demon. Stories told in Noh plays are acted out through music, dance and gestures instead of dialogue. One famous story is about a princess called Kiyohime and the priest who wronged her.

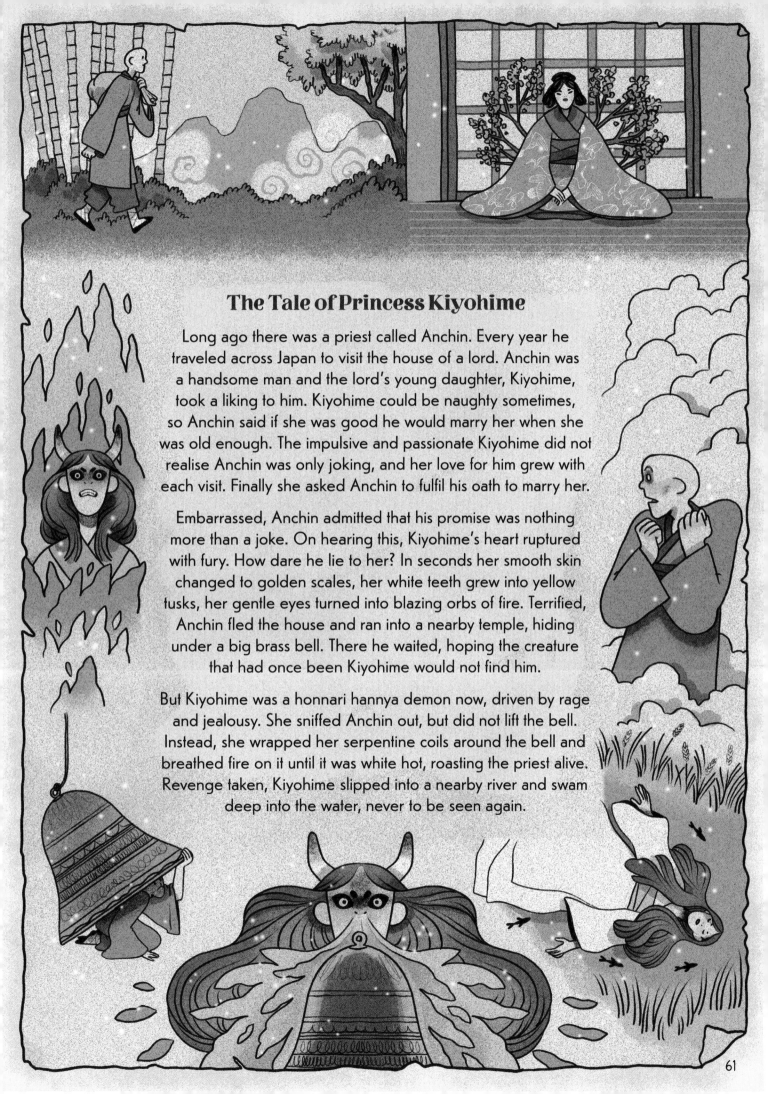

The Tale of Princess Kiyohime

Long ago there was a priest called Anchin. Every year he traveled across Japan to visit the house of a lord. Anchin was a handsome man and the lord's young daughter, Kiyohime, took a liking to him. Kiyohime could be naughty sometimes, so Anchin said if she was good he would marry her when she was old enough. The impulsive and passionate Kiyohime did not realise Anchin was only joking, and her love for him grew with each visit. Finally she asked Anchin to fulfil his oath to marry her.

Embarrassed, Anchin admitted that his promise was nothing more than a joke. On hearing this, Kiyohime's heart ruptured with fury. How dare he lie to her? In seconds her smooth skin changed to golden scales, her white teeth grew into yellow tusks, her gentle eyes turned into blazing orbs of fire. Terrified, Anchin fled the house and ran into a nearby temple, hiding under a big brass bell. There he waited, hoping the creature that had once been Kiyohime would not find him.

But Kiyohime was a honnari hannya demon now, driven by rage and jealousy. She sniffed Anchin out, but did not lift the bell. Instead, she wrapped her serpentine coils around the bell and breathed fire on it until it was white hot, roasting the priest alive. Revenge taken, Kiyohime slipped into a nearby river and swam deep into the water, never to be seen again.

EUROPEAN WITCH-HUNTERS
1500–1800

King James VI of Scotland sits at a desk, tapping a quill against his chin. In front of him lies a parchment. The ornate calligraphy at the top reads: "An Act against Conjuration, Witchcraft and Dealing with Evil and Wicked Spirits." The nib scratches as he signs his name. Red ink pools like blood.

Welcome to early modern Europe

Many societies respected their magic-users, but not in Europe between the 16th and 18th centuries. At that time, being a witch was a very dangerous occupation. The Catholic church's attitude towards witches became deeply suspicious and hostile. They preached to the population that sorcery was an act against God, and that witches gained their powers through pacts with the Church's worst enemy: the Devil.

Witch-hunting

During the medieval period, witches had been able to work and live in relative peace. Now, the Pope and his priests proclaimed that they were evil and had to be rooted out and destroyed. A witch-hunting craze spread across Europe. Ordinary people who once went to their local witch for medical advice now screamed "Heresy!" at them, before turning them over to the witch-hunters.

Anti-witchcraft laws

The Church's increasing hostility meant laws changed, making life harder for witches. In the 1563 Act Against Conjurations, Enchantments and Witchcrafts in England, anyone who used magic faced the death penalty, but only if the magic caused harm. Attitudes towards witches were much harsher in Scotland. The Scottish Witchcraft Act of 1563 stated that all witches, and anyone who consulted with them, should be put to death even if the magic was being used for good.

In Europe, many witch hunters and judges used a book called the *Malleus Maleficarum* (page 66-67) as a guide to finding and punishing witches. France, Switzerland, Norway, Denmark and Germany went through waves of witch persecutions. Witches, and anyone who dared use their services, lived in constant fear of accusation. Some estimates say that thousands of people (mostly women) were executed after being accused of witchcraft.

By the mid-1700s, the witch-hunting craze across Europe had started to die down. New laws such as the Witchcraft Act of 1735 were passed, undoing the previous laws in England and Scotland that had caused so much terror. However, European settlers in North America were slow to catch up in their attitudes towards witches, leading to one of the most notorious prosecutions in history: the Salem Witch Trials.

THE SALEM WITCH TRIALS

In 1692, in a small village in America called Salem, two young girls—Betty Parris and her cousin Abigail Williams—began acting very oddly. Frightened witnesses said the girls screamed, twisted their bodies and complained of being bitten by unseen forces. Their affliction soon spread to other villagers, and even church sermons were interrupted by people convulsing and crying out. Doctors couldn't explain it, and so the people blamed witchcraft.

There were three women in Salem who were social outcasts, and they were accused of using dark magic to curse Betty and Abigail. Soon, a witch-hunting craze swept like a plague across the village. Once arrested, people were given no legal help and little time to prepare their defence. Many people who were arrested accused others of witchcraft in an effort to save themselves from punishment. Panic spread quickly.

At that time, people believed in "spectral evidence," where the victims of sorcery saw their witch-tormentors in nightmares. It is likely that people lied about having such nightmares to falsely blame their enemies.

Of the estimated two hundred people arrested, over 20 were executed. After a year, the witch-hunting frenzy passed. The trials ended and people began to question how such a strange and terrible event could have ever taken place. Even today, people still remember the unjust and infamous Salem Witch Trials.

MALLEUS MALEFICARUM

Malleus Maleficarum is Latin for "Hammer of Witches"—a suitably violent name for a book that taught witch-hunters how to find and destroy magic-users. The book was written in the 1480s by Catholic clergyman Heinrich Kramer, who believed that witches were evil. He split his gruesome book into three sections.

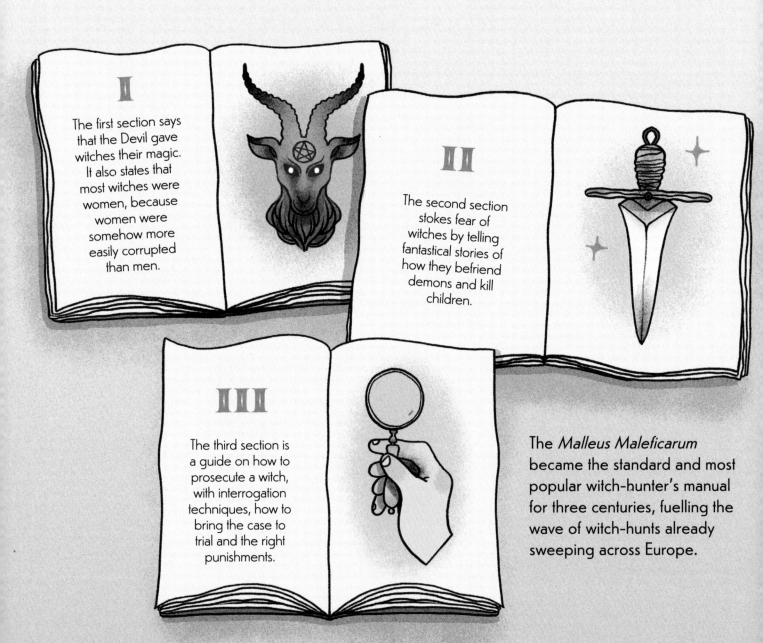

I

The first section says that the Devil gave witches their magic. It also states that most witches were women, because women were somehow more easily corrupted than men.

II

The second section stokes fear of witches by telling fantastical stories of how they befriend demons and kill children.

III

The third section is a guide on how to prosecute a witch, with interrogation techniques, how to bring the case to trial and the right punishments.

The *Malleus Maleficarum* became the standard and most popular witch-hunter's manual for three centuries, fuelling the wave of witch-hunts already sweeping across Europe.

Ways to catch a witch

Here are some despicable methods witch-hunters used to "prove" that people were witches:

Water test

The witch-hunter tied the suspected witch's thumb to her toe and threw her into a river. If she floated, it "proved" that she was a witch because the water rejected her. If she sank, it meant the water accepted her, so she wasn't a witch. Either way, it did not end well for the accused person.

False familiar

The suspect was locked in a room under careful watch. If an animal—a rat, mouse, or even a fly—entered the room it was assumed to be the witch's familiar coming to help her, thus "proving" she was a witch.

Pricking

It was believed that magic-users had a "witch's mark," a small skin blemish that felt no pain and never bled. If the person didn't cry out when the blemish was jabbed with a needle, it meant they were a witch. Witch-hunters were paid per witch they found, so they may have used blunt or retractable needles to jab suspects and claim the reward.

Walking

Some witch-hunters forced confessions by making the suspect walk endlessly in a circle without stopping, sometimes for days. They were denied food, water and sleep until they broke down from exhaustion. Desperate suspects often gave false confessions to make the torment stop.

MODERN DAY MAGIC
1900-present day

Moonlight shimmers on the sea. By the shore, a group gather around a fire, chanting and singing, their arms raised upwards. Flames shoot sparks into the darkness to whirl and dance like fireflies. Inside the flickering light, happiness grows. The Moon Goddess smiles.

Welcome to now!

The practice of witchcraft in Europe declined between the 18th and the early 20th centuries as the age of scientific discovery progressed. New medical techniques meant that ancient beliefs in the healing powers of magic were no longer respected. However, in the early 1900s, interest in witchcraft grew again. Modern Western witchcraft is now a wide and varied practice. Many branches of modern witchcraft, like Wicca, use ancient pre-Christian religions as a basis for their beliefs. There is often a focus on protecting nature, maintaining balance in the world and healing the mind, body and spirit.

Wicca

The modern practice of Wicca teaches that humans should live in harmony with nature. Wiccans worship two gods: the Moon Goddess and the Horned God (sometimes called the Lady and the Lord). The Moon Goddess is connected to the Moon, the stars and the sea. She looks after the souls of the dead and gives love to the living. The Horned God is connected to the Sun and to the wilderness, representing hunting and the cycle of life and death.

Magic circles

Wiccans practice white magic using magic circles, which are created by a High Priestess or Priest. First, the space for the magic circle is purified with a sweep of a broom. Then, the Priestess or Priest walks around the edge of the circle, using their magic to give it power. Sometimes they use a wand or ceremonial knife held in the air to create the circle. Four points, set an equal distance apart, are marked on the edge with lit candles. These represent the four natural elements of fire, air, water and earth. The most important factor when making a magic circle is the belief of the participants and the skill of the High Priestess or Priest.

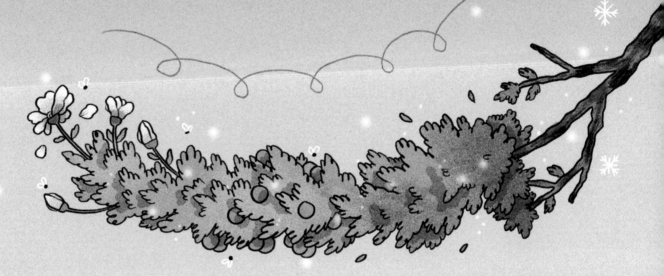

Seasonal solstice

Wiccans celebrate the seasonal festivals of the summer and winter solstices (the longest and shortest days of the year), and the spring and autumn equinoxes (when day and night are of equal length). The solstices and equinoxes have been celebrated as important days for thousands of years because they mark important changes in nature and the weather. Wiccans believe that magic is particularly strong at the time of the summer solstice.

GERALD GARDNER

Father of Wicca

Wicca was developed in England by writer and archaeologist Gerald Gardner. He was also an anthropologist, which meant that he studied people and their histories. While working as a government official in Ceylon (now known as Sri Lanka) and Malaya (now known as Malaysia) in the early 1900s, he became interested in the indigenous peoples' magical practices.

Gardner moved back to England in 1936 and joined a secretive coven (a group of witches) in the New Forest. He used their faith in witchcraft, ceremonial magic and ancient pre-Christian gods as a basis for his own belief system, which would later become known as Wicca—from the word for "witch" in Old English.

Gardner needed lots of people to join his religion to make it thrive, so he tirelessly spread the word about his "Craft of the Wise." He recruited High Priestesses to start their own covens and lead magical ceremonies. He also appeared on television and wrote several books. In time, Wicca gained followers in Britain, Australia and the USA, and Gardner became known as the "Father of Wicca." He died in 1964 at the age of 79. His gravestone is marked with the words "Beloved of the Great Goddess."

The Tale Continues...

A SILVER THREAD

*Embers and smoke drift from the dying campfire.
All the tales have been told, and it's time for the witches
to go home. They disappear between the trees, back to
their places in history. Each leaves a trail of silver magic
in the air, dancing like dust in the light of the moon.*

And now, we've reached the end of our tale. There is much more to know about magic and its users than what lies within these pages (we would need a much bigger book!), but now we can understand magic's place in our history. For centuries, people have tried to improve their lives by magical means, and that magic runs through our history like a silver thread.

We've seen that witches were as varied as the cultures and times they sprang from. While some worked in magnificent temples, others scraped a living in forest caves. While some were highly valued by their societies, others were shunned and despised.

Fewer people believe in magic these days, although it still has a powerful hold on our imaginations. Whether you believe magic is real or not, the cultures and civilizations you've read about here most certainly did. It was as much a part of their world as the air they breathed — invisible, yes, but very real.

This book is dedicated to all magic-users of the past, present and future: the witches, warlocks and wise women, the sorcerers, sangomas and shamans, the völvur, vodou queens and all magical folk who saw further and deeper than ordinary people dare to look.

INDEX

ISBN: 978-1-912497-71-3

www.flyingeyebooks.com

More magic from Flying Eye Books...

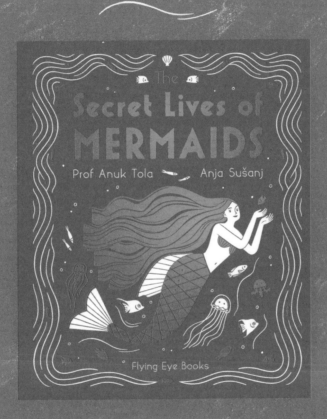

The
Secret Lives of
MERMAIDS

Prof Anuk Tola   Anja Sušanj

Flying Eye Books

For the first time, everything that humans have learned about mermaids has been written down — and now you can discover it too! Famed merologist Professor Anuk Tola has dedicated her life to learning about these mysterious and playful creatures. From how they swim so fast to what a mermaid family looks like, uncover a kingdom of secret mermaid knowledge in this stunningly illustrated guide.